Tackling domestic violence:
A guide to developing multi-ager

The Domestic Violence Research Group at the University of Bristol con   ʒ.ɔnal and
international studies of policy and practice issues related to domestic vio.   .. ɪ ne group liaises
closely with WAFE, the Women's Aid Federation of England.

This guide has been prepared by the Domestic Violence Research Group as part of a two year
national study of multi-agency responses to domestic violence, generously supported by the Joseph
Rowntree Foundation.

The Domestic Violence Research Group is independent, and the views expressed in this pack do not
necessarily reflect those of WAFE, of the Research Advisory Group to the study, or of any one
agency.

The Women's Aid Federation of England (WAFE) is the key national agency in England promoting
the protection of women and children experiencing domestic violence, monitoring policy and
practice on domestic violence and coordinating the provision of refuges, support and advocacy
services. WAFE is one of four national Women's Aid federations (together with Scottish Women's
Aid, Welsh Women's Aid and Northern Ireland Women's Aid). All the federations have a training
and consultancy role in developing strategies regarding multi-agency coordination. WAFE, in
particular, has provided support and training to many new and established multi-agency initiatives.

The research study which gave rise to this guide, was conducted between 1994 and 1996 by Gill
Hague, Ellen Malos and Wendy Dear.

It resulted in the publication of:

> A 1996 national report, *Multi-agency work and domestic violence: A national study of inter-
> agency initiatives*, by Gill Hague, Ellen Malos and Wendy Dear, published by The Policy
> Press.

> A Joseph Rowntree Foundation Findings, entitled *Inter-agency Initiatives as a Response to
> Domestic Violence*, Social Policy Research 101, June 1996.

> A 1995 working paper, *Against Domestic Violence: Inter-agency Initiatives*, by Gill Hague,
> Ellen Malos and Wendy Dear, published by SAUS publications, University of Bristol.

*The guide can be used in conjunction with these publications. It has been compiled to act as a quick and
practical guide, and does not contain a discussion of policy or of the wider and complex issues involved in
multi-agency work on domestic violence. Issues covered arise specifically from the research study. Thus, the
publication relates to findings from the research rather than presenting comprehensive resource and
practice guidance.*

Contents

Acknowledgements

This resource pack was produced independently, however it arose from a national study of multi-agency responses to domestic violence, funded by the Joseph Rowntree Foundation, and conducted by the authors, together with our colleague, Wendy Dear, to whom we are most grateful. We are indebted to the Joseph Rowntree Foundation for their generous financial and professional support of the original study and to the members of the Research Advisory Group to the study: Barbara Ballard, Joseph Rowntree Foundation; Olwen Edwards, Nottinghamshire Inter-agency Domestic Violence Forum; Joan Evans, Enfield Women's Aid; Jane Geraghty, South Yorkshire Probation Service; Nicola Harwin, Women's Aid Federation (England); Rebecca Morley, University of Nottingham; Audrey Mullender, University of Durham; Lorna Smith, Home Office; Andrea Tara-Chand, Leeds Inter-agency Project; Monica Townsend, Crown Prosecution Service; Annette Young, Department of Health.

Special thanks are due to Nicola Harwin for her comments on this guide. Thanks are also due to a variety of practitioners and organisations who made comments and contributions. We are particularly grateful to Charlene Henry, Hadhari Nari Centre, Derby; Robyn Holder, formerly of London Borough of Hammersmith and Fulham Community Safety Unit; Davina James-Hanman, London Borough of Islington Women's Equality Unit; Gill Roberts, Welsh Women's Aid; Ann Wardell, Cleveland Multi-agency Domestic Violence Forum and Ann Webster, Derby City Council Equalities Unit. We would like to thank Myra Johnson of The Policy Press for her assistance and support.

1 How to use the guide

This guide has been designed as a simple and easy to read guide to multi-agency domestic violence work. It has been prepared to be of use both to established domestic violence initiatives and new multi-agency groups just starting out. The pack can be used by women's refuge and advocacy services, the police, local authorities, other statutory and voluntary sector agencies, private firms (for example, solicitors), domestic violence forum coordinators and management bodies, and women and children experiencing domestic violence. Each section leads on to the next stage. However the sections can be used separately to provide brief guidance to the issues involved.

Definitions:

While the term 'inter-agency' is widely used in domestic violence circles, the term 'multi-agency' more properly explains the type of cooperation between agencies which is current in domestic violence work. Therefore for the purposes of this guide we have used the term 'multi-agency' throughout.

2 The multi-agency approach to domestic violence

The multi-agency approach to dealing with domestic violence has been recommended by a wide range of bodies and groups, both nationally and internationally. Examples include:

- The 1992 National Inter-Agency Working Party Report, *Domestic Violence*, produced by Victim Support with the active collaboration of other agencies including Women's Aid Federation (England) (WAFE).

- The 1993 House of Commons Home Affairs Committee Report of the *Inquiry into Domestic Violence*.

- The 1993 *Government Reply* to this Inquiry Report.

The police, in particular, have been encouraged to engage in multi-agency work on domestic violence by the Home Office, for example in sections of *Home Officer Circular 60/ 1990*.

The government has recently established inter-departmental Ministerial and Officials groups to develop policy on domestic violence, with the Home Office being identified as the lead agency. One result of these initiatives is that multi-agency approaches to domestic violence were the subject of a major Home Office Inter-agency Circular published in 1995. The Circular is entitled: *Inter-agency Coordination to Tackle Domestic Violence*.

It recommends that all relevant agencies work together to coordinate their responses to domestic violence.

What are multi-agency domestic violence initiatives?

Multi-agency initiatives as a response to domestic violence take a wide variety of forms.

- Some consist of discrete or one-off projects, for example, setting up a particular domestic violence training course on a multi-agency basis.

- Most commonly, they take the form of an on-going domestic violence forum. Domestic violence forums aim to bring together all the agencies in the locality to form a coordinated response to domestic violence. At least 200 forums of this type existed in 1996.

- In some areas, multi-agency work may occur, but in a much less formalised way. It may consist of long-established informal liaison between agencies and can be just as successful as a more formal arrangements.

No two multi-agency domestic violence initiatives are the same. They cannot be slotted into distinct models or categories.

Multi-agency coordination needs to evolve organically from local circumstances. What works well in one area may not work in another.

This resource pack is concerned with the work of domestic violence forums and other similar initiatives, although it may also be of help where liaison is more informal.

3 Who is involved?

The first stage in setting up a domestic violence forum is to get the commitment and involvement of as comprehensive a range of statutory and voluntary sector agencies as possible; providing that they have some involvement in domestic violence work.

Both **statutory** and **voluntary sector agencies**, including Women's Aid and the refuge movement, need to be involved.

Relevant agencies and individuals include:

Women's Aid refuges, the Women's Aid federations, and other refuges including specialist refuges, for example, refuges for black women and children or for women and children from minority ethnic communities, and women's advocacy and support services

The police

The probation service

Local authority specialist units where these exist (eg, community safety or women's equality units)

Local authority social services departments

Local authority housing departments

Local authority education departments

Housing associations and other relevant housing bodies

Health services and health care providers

Victim Support

Women's and community organisations

Other voluntary sector agencies

Solicitors

Crown prosecution service

Judges and magistrates

Legal and court personnel

Women who have experienced domestic violence.

4 How to get started

One or more agencies need to take the initiative. Most commonly, the initiating organisations are the police, Women's Aid and other refuges and women's services, the probation service, the local authority (often through a specialist unit within it, for example, a community safety unit) or Victim Support.

It does not matter which agency takes the initiative as long as that agency does not dominate the work or 'own' the project or the work done.

Ideas for getting going

- Call a meeting or workshop of relevant agencies or a series of meetings and workshops about setting up a domestic violence forum, or organise a local or regional conference or seminar specifically to discuss setting up a forum.

- When you have agreed to set up a forum, establish a working group to get the initiative moving.

- Form an on-going forum with a commitment to holding regular meetings involving all member agencies.

- Consider engaging together in some initial domestic violence training to raise awareness about the issue and to balance different agencies' knowledge about domestic violence.

- Try to avoid any one agency dominating proceedings (although initially one or two agencies often have to take the initiative and put in energy in order to maintain and develop interest from others).

- Consider contacting the relevant Women's Aid federation or other consultants for assistance, especially if there is not a refuge in the area.

A few general points

- Many new forums set up an initial series of meetings, each of which has an agreed theme or topic.

- It is helpful if agencies attending try to develop clarity about why they are there and their role in the group.

- It is important that both statutory and voluntary sector agencies attend meetings.

- There is a need for independent women's advocacy representation in domestic violence work. Refuges and women's support services in the locality need to be involved from the beginning.

- Even where meetings are informal; chairing and minute taking are useful.

Once you have agreed to set up a multi-agency forum, you need to consider what jobs or tasks need to be taken on.

Some initial tasks

- Get to know each other.

- Share experiences about domestic violence work.

- Agree initial tasks and agendas.

- Organise chairing and servicing arrangements.

- Make sure all the relevant agencies are invited.

- Draw up a mailing list.

- Discuss attitudes and ideas about domestic violence.

- Identify and discuss gaps in services.

- Discuss a role for any ongoing forum, possible activities and informal aims and objectives.

Action Points

☐ Are all the agencies involved who ought to be?

☐ Are both voluntary and statutory agencies present?

☐ Are local refuges or other women's advocacy services involved?

☐ Is there a useful role for a forum?

☐ Have abused women been consulted or involved in any way?

☐ Is the group dominated by any one agency?

☐ Are there any resources?

Ideas on how to service a forum

- Agencies can share servicing and resourcing tasks initially. For example, one agency might provide the venue for all meetings, or another might regularly take the minutes.

- Agencies can rotate servicing and secretarial tasks and venues for meetings between them. For example, meetings could be organised and minuted by a different agency each time.

- One agency might have the resources to provide on-going servicing and administrative assistance, for example the local authority or the police.

Police-initiated forums

As a result of Home Office and police guidance, local police services have set up many domestic violence forums throughout the country. In fact, as formal 'initiators' the policy have taken a more active role than any other one agency. Because of conflicts between the police and some other agencies and criticisms of some aspects of policing, forums initiated by the police worked best where:

- The police do not dominate proceedings.

- The police do not chair all meetings or control agendas.

- The group does not meet in police stations.

- Dedicated domestic violence units or domestic violence officer posts are in existence.

- Refuges, women's advocacy and support services, and the voluntary sector, are fully involved.

5 Networking

Most multi-agency initiatives begin as networking groups, although some start off with a specific urgent piece of work which is the catalyst to agencies coming together. In networking groups, agencies get to know each other, exchange information and ideas, and learn from each other about domestic violence. Many domestic violence forums stay as networking groups throughout their existence.

Advantages	Disadvantages
Networking groups can:	Networking groups may:
Help agencies and individuals to get to know each other.	Become a 'talking shop' and nothing more.
Break down barriers and misunderstandings between agencies.	Reach a period of stagnation and lack of interest.
Build trust and confidence between agencies.	Waste valuable time and resources.
Help to educate and learn about each other.	
Give support to each other.	Use the expertise of some agencies (eg, refuges) as informal training without acknowledging the strain that this can place on the resources of such agencies or compensating them in any way.
Enable agencies to share experiences and examples of good practice.	
Begin the process of identifying unmet needs of women and children experiencing domestic violence.	Duplicate discussions (especially if different people attend each meeting).
Identify gaps and overlaps in services.	
Improve liaison, referrals and joint practice between agencies.	

However, networking between agencies, getting to know each other and educating each other about each agency's work has value in itself. This is particularly the case when issues of relevance to the safety and needs of abused women and children stay central, and repetitive discussions are avoided.

Many domestic violence forums choose to engage in joint activities, as well as networking, but this is only possible if the conditions are right.

Without the will to develop further and without resourcing of some sort, it is very difficult for groups to move on from networking to service coordination and other work. Group members need to have the available time and energy to develop the group further.

Thus, two key needs for further development are:

• Resources

• Commitment and time

6   How to move on from networking

A: Making decisions

Many multi-agency initiatives decide to take a role in coordinating and improving local practice on domestic violence. If you decide to move on from being solely a networking group in this way you need to work out ways of:

- reaching agreement

- making decisions

- resolving differences between agencies

Some ideas on how to reach decisions and resolve differences

- Work out practical methods for reaching agreement and for dealing with differences of opinion.

- In some situations, agree to differ, but be clear about exactly what the areas of disagreement and agreement are.

- Take on power differences and variations in levels of resources between agencies.

- Make sure that the perspectives and interests of women and children who have experienced domestic violence remain central.

- Make sure that in resolving differences of opinion between agencies and between individuals, the forum does not resort to a 'lowest common denominator' situation.

- Use good communication skills, reasoned debate and openness to honesty and challenge. This can mean avoiding the tendency of individual agencies to 'defend their own turf'.

- If necessary, make use of facilitators, consultants and specialist training provision on:

  domestic violence
  multi-agency working
  communication skills
  team building

- Where possible, make decisions by consensus, making sure that all agencies are able to participate equally in discussions and feel equally welcome and involved.

- Acknowledge shared responsibility for making decisions and for the success (or difficulties) of the forum so that its work, activities and development are 'owned' by all members.

Two useful points to remember

- Because multi-agency work is very complex, clarity between all members is essential in relation to decision making, processes and procedures. For example:

  who can make decisions about what?

  who controls resources?

- The effectiveness of decision making needs to be monitored regularly, as do any special techniques used to involve all members and assist decision making.

However, resolving difference so that the agencies can engage in productive work together is one of the most difficult issues facing domestic violence forums and initiatives.

Disagreements often surface about understandings of domestic violence and about the gender issues involved.

Women's Aid and the refuge network throughout the country have been providing independent advocacy for abused women and children, and developing expertise on domestic violence for more than 20 years. In fact, the Women's Aid federations and refuges are now acknowledged as the lead specialist agencies dealing with domestic violence.

It therefore makes sense if their views and ethos are integrated into multi-agency work. The approaches to domestic violence which they have developed can usefully inform agreements developed by domestic violence forums, even where there is no refuge in the local area, for example:

- The empowerment of abused women and children.

- The centrality of the views and needs of women experiencing domestic violence.

- Understanding domestic violence based on concepts of control and of power in relationships between men and women.

The *Duluth Model* is widely used in domestic violence training and multi-agency work. This model is based on ideas about developing a coordinated, multi-faceted community response to domestic violence and uses a power and control analysis of domestic violence. It was developed by the Duluth Abuse Intervention Project in Duluth, Minnesota. Information about it can be obtained from domestic violence trainers and consultants, from multi-agency projects who are using it, from the Women's Aid federations, from domestic violence researchers, and from many publications.

One way of reaching agreements about philosophy and ethos is the develop written **principles, aims** and **vision** or **a mission statement**. These agreements can give forums focus and direction and give member agencies something to 'sign up' to.

B.   Developing written agreements

Some ideas

Written agreements can:

- Give domestic violence forums focus and direction.

- Help to resolve disagreements.

- Give participating agencies something to 'sign up' to.

- Bring clarity and purpose to the whole endeavour.

Develop a set of guiding principles to which all can agree

These may include agreements on:

- Defining domestic violence.

- Working to oppose domestic violence and viewing it as a crime.

- Having a commitment to increase the safety of women experiencing domestic violence and their children.

- Having a commitment to reduce the level and impact of domestic violence.

- Integrating equalities issues into the work of the forum.

Example of guiding principles (I)

1. Accepting that domestic violence is a crime and is unacceptable in our community.

2. The services available to a woman should be offered in a non-judgmental way and should aim to maximise her choices.

3. Mutual respect, trust, professionalism and a desire for sensitive and appropriate service delivery are essential to our collaboration.

4. Respect for the accountability of each agency's representatives to their own management group.

Example of guiding principles (II) (from a county-wide forum)

1. To function as a Forum for information exchange between agencies in order to provide victims of domestic violence with the necessary advice and support.

2 To co-ordinate county-wide initiatives and ad hoc projects.

3. To encourage agencies to develop a code of practice for dealing with domestic violence (which respects area policy on responding to domestic violence).

4. To maintain an active and productive approach to multi-agency working.

5. To support and maintain the autonomy of local groups and facilitate local initiatives.

Agree formal aims and objectives

After drawing up guiding principles, many forums move on to formulate a set of broad aims and more detailed objectives. Improving the safety of abused women and children needs to be primary among these, but some forums overlook this basic commitment.

Example of aims and objectives (I)

To continue developing and implementing an inter-agency strategy on domestic violence which seeks:

1. To promote and maintain cooperation and joint action.

2. To increase awareness of domestic violence in the community and agencies.

3. To improve services and responses to women and children who have experienced or are experiencing domestic violence.

4. To take positive action against perpetrators.

5. To maximise the resources available to promote the above.

Example of aims and objectives (II) (from a county-wide forum)

1. To raise the awareness and profile of domestic violence locally.

2. To identify and pool resource needs and raise finance for county-wide initiatives.

3. To promote multi-agency training throughout the county.

4. To respond to a local, national and international agenda on domestic violence and to develop links with other projects.

5. To identify differences between areas in their response to domestic violence by sharing and exchanging information, in order to influence the delivery of quality services in the county.

Example of aims and objectives (III)

1. To increase knowledge and awareness within agencies of domestic violence.

2. To provide opportunities for interaction between agencies including the voluntary sector, and build trust and co-operation between agencies.

3. To influence agencies to improve, promote and co-ordinate their services to women experiencing domestic violence.

4. To provide information to people affected by domestic violence. To research the needs of women in order to identify gaps in services.

5. To inform and educate the wider community on domestic violence issues and campaign where appropriate.

6. To review the work and terms of reference of the Forum on a regular basis.

To further strengthen these agreements, formulate:

Detailed terms of reference

These may include:

- Mission or vision statements

- Equal opportunity policies

- Procedural guidelines

- Any other agreed procedures and statements

Example of an equal opportunities policy

1. The Forum, its work and service delivery, will ensure that equal opportunities are incorporated at all stages, and will not discriminate on the basis of colour, race, gender, nationality, sexual preference, marital status, age, class, disability/ability, religious or political beliefs.

2. The forum recognises that black agencies / people are under-represented in the Forum. The Forum will encourage and seek the participation and involvement of black agencies / people through positive action and by the formation of anti-racist strategies and active recruitment of black members to the Forum.

3. The Forum will also encourage and seek the participation and involvement of other groups and people who may experience discrimination on those grounds outlined in paragraph 1.

Example of a mission statement

1. It is the intention of the Forum to bring about social change with regard to domestic violence, the treatment of people experiencing domestic violence and the treatment of perpetrators.

2. Our mission statement is as follows:

To achieve the general acceptance that domestic violence is a crime and unacceptable to society, to ensure that support is given to people experiencing domestic violence and help for perpetrators is readily available and accessible.

Example of procedural guidelines

1. Membership of the Forum is open to any interested group, organisation or individual willing to adhere to the Terms of Reference and Equal Opportunities Policy and to assist the Forum in progressing its aims.

2. The Forum is expected to meet a minimum of four times per annum.

3. The Forum meetings will be chaired by the Co-ordinator.

4. All members are expected to participate on sub-committees or working parties established to achieve strategic objectives and progress the aims of the group.

5. Particular reference should be made to the Equal Opportunities Policy in all aspects of work undertaken by the Forum.

6. Members of the Forum should seek to address the role and position of all women in society in all aspects of work undertaken.

Two action points

- All terms of reference, and equal opportunity policies in particular, need to be *monitored* and *reviewed* regularly.

- It can be helpful if participating agencies *make written agreements that they accept* the principles and terms of reference of the forum.

As a forum develops a clear remit it may be helpful to agree mechanisms to ensure that the focus is not lost or diluted by the presence of agencies without a related contribution to make. Sometimes a smaller, focused forum can complete pieces of work more efficiently than a larger, less focused one.

C.   Developing an operating structure

As domestic violence multi-agency initiatives start taking a role in service coordination, members may find that making all decisions in the full forum meetings can be difficult. This can be overcome by developing a working structure, although for small forums this may be unnecessary or inappropriate.

Clarity between participating agencies about the role of each agency and what each can contribute can be of assistance in developing such a structure.

Typically, domestic violence forums meet regularly as a full group, perhaps every few months, but it is useful to establish:

A steering group or committee

A steering group or committee will manage the work of the forum and take responsibility for its day-to-day running. Thus, steering groups may resemble voluntary sector project management committees.

It is helpful if steering group members have the stated commitment and backing of their agency.

A steering committee needs:

- To contain representatives of a range of active agencies in the forum.

- Where possible, to include both voluntary and statutory sector representatives.

- Where possible, to include representatives of local refuges, advocacy and support services, other women's projects and of minority groups and communities.

- To be elected, if possible, often with formal officer posts, for a set time period.

- To be accountable to the full membership.

- To develop clear procedures and lines of accountability.

- To have an active and consistent membership.

- To take responsibility for managing any employees unless these are employed through a statutory or other body.

- To meet more often than the full forum.

- To develop specific job or role descriptions for officers and members of the committee, for example, the chair.

Example of a job description of a Chairperson for a Steering Committee

Duties and responsibilities

1. Planning and running meetings ensuring everything is covered and decisions are made when required.

2. Keeping order.

3. Helping the Committee deal with differences of opinion and conflicts.

4. Being sure that everyone has a chance to speak who wants to.

5. Ensuring the Steering Committee as a whole makes and sticks to its policies and priorities.

6. Acting as a spokesperson for the Committee, making essential or emergency decisions between Committee Meetings.

7. Helping any worker deal with difficult situations.

8. Acting as Line Manager to the Co-ordinator, which will include:

    - authorising annual leave, days off in lieu, attendance at training courses, seminars etc.

    - conducting 3 monthly staff appraisal sessions with the Co-ordinator.

    - dealing with any difficulties the Co-ordinator may have.

9. Liaising regularly with the Vice Chairperson should they need to stand in at short notice.

Domestic violence forums may also set up sub-groups in addition to, or instead of, a steering group.

Sub-groups may have a general brief, for example, a legal, housing or children's sub-group. Alternatively, they may have a specific remit, for example, to organise a conference or to develop a set of practice guidelines.

A sub-group needs:

- To have a consistent and active membership.

- To be possibly time limited in its total duration or to ask members to serve for a set time to enable agency representatives to take part for a manageable time period.

- To be task-oriented.

- To have a clear remit.

- To be accountable to the full forum or to the Steering Group.

- To have access to agreed resources and to be clear about how, when and why these resources may be accessed.

What about the wider structure?

- Many multi-agency initiatives have not developed constitutions.

- Some forums are set up and constituted as voluntary sector projects, as limited companies or as charities.

- Some are connected to, or 'hosted' by, a statutory agency.

- Some remain as networks of concerned organisations.

Advice on drawing up constitutions, becoming a limited company, applying for charitable status, and so forth, is available from the relevant professional organisations and accredited bodies.

Different ways of organising domestic violence forums will have implications for how any employees are employed and managed.

Action plans

Once basic agreements have been reached and a working structure has been established, many forums go on to develop:

Detailed action plans

Action plans are detailed lists of activities and goals to be achieved in a given time-scale, for example, over a year.

- Activities included need to be achievable in the period covered by the action plan.

- Action plans may be reviewed for progress in each area of work included at every forum meeting, or at regular meetings.

Longer established forums may go on to develop:

Longer-term strategic plans

- Longer-term strategic plans (eg, for three or five years) can provide a framework of goals, plans and development of services.

- For well-established initiatives, a lack of strategic planning can hamper planning and forward development.

7 Types of work done by multi-agency forums

Beyond networking, domestic violence multi-agency forums engage in five main types of work. These are:

- Coordinating local agency responses and services in relation to domestic violence.
- Improving the practice of agencies and service delivery.
- Setting up new projects to assist women experiencing domestic violence and their children, and supporting refuges and existing projects.
- Engaging in public education and awareness raising work about domestic violence.
- Engaging in preventative and general educational work.

A. Coordinating local services

This includes a wide-range of activities depending on local needs. Some examples are:

- Producing resource directories and guides for agencies.
- Initiating improvements in referral systems and liaison between agencies.
- Hosting multi-agency conferences, meetings and training events.
- Monitoring domestic violence referrals and practice across agencies throughout the locality.

B. Improving agency practice and service delivery

This includes contributing to the evolution of domestic violence policies and practice guidance and developing domestic violence training. Some examples are:

- Identifying particular, unmet needs of women and their children who are experiencing domestic violence in the area.
- Conducting small-scale local research projects in a 'woman-centred' way, for example, on the specific needs of black women or lesbians experiencing domestic violence.
- Conducting a service audit of the domestic violence services offered by all local agencies, in conjunction with these agencies, to identify examples of good practice, gaps in services etc. As a result, working with individual agencies to assist them in drawing up individual agency action plans.
- Formulating and agreeing multi-agency practice guidelines which all member agencies can then adopt.
- In a consultative role, assisting individual agencies in evolving their own detailed domestic violence policies and good practice guidance.

It can also be important for local forums to take a role in ensuring that domestic violence is taken on as an issue by other new or existing community or agency projects with a different remit. Domestic violence is often overlooked in these contexts.

Thus, multi-agency projects can act as:

- An advisory or consultative body on domestic violence issues in a locality.

- A 'watchdog' on the quality of local services, taking up examples of bad practice and supporting the interests of women and children experiencing domestic violence.

Multi-agency domestic violence training

One of the most important ways in which multi-agency forums can assist member and other agencies to improve their practice is to provide domestic violence training.

Many domestic violence forums now offer training to local agencies.

Training may:

- Be developed and delivered by multi-agency initiatives through a training sub-group.

- Include both domestic violence awareness training and material on the implementation of policy and practice.

- Be delivered on a cascade 'Training the Trainers' model where officers are trained, often using outside consultants and trainers initially, and can then train others.

- Be offered to either multi-agency or single-agency groups.

Current good practice in domestic violence training

- Training needs to have an underlying focus on meeting the needs of women and children experiencing domestic violence and improving their safety.

- The views and perspectives of abused women can usefully inform training sessions in a direct way. Survivors of domestic violence are sometimes involved in developing and delivering training.

- All training needs to be sensitive to cultural, race, class, disability and sexuality issues. It also needs to include the development of anti-discriminatory practice and equalities work as an integral part of the material offered, rather than something which is 'added on'.

- Multi-agency forums should not duplicate or take over the training which is already being offered by Women's Aid and other refuges.

- There needs to be clarity about payment for training offered and about who 'owns' any training resources developed.

- Training can usefully be targeted towards specific group of workers, including managers as well as front-line practitioners.

- Training needs to be monitored to gauge its effectiveness and to identify future training needs.

C. Setting up new services and projects for abused women and children and supporting existing refuges and women's advocacy and support services

- Setting up women's support groups and drop-in services, advice lines, children's projects and other new services.

- Linking new services developed by multi-agency forums to existing independent refuge, advocacy and support services, where possible.

- Acting to facilitate the development and resourcing of refuges and outreach projects, and of women's support services locally.

- Acting directly to support funding applications from such services.

- Assisting in obtaining resources which can further expand the role of refuges, advocacy and support services in order to develop multi-agency coordination and outreach, where possible, rather than setting up projects in competition.

It should be noted that relatively few domestic violence forums set up new projects of their own. Many focus instead on coordinating services and on engaging in educational, awareness-raising and preventative work.

D. Engaging in public education and awareness raising work

This includes:

- Running local Zero Tolerance campaigns (a type of public awareness campaign initiated in Edinburgh) or other public awareness campaigns.

- Producing leaflets, information packs and general information material for the use of women and children experiencing domestic violence.

- Producing leaflets, booklets and posters to educate the general public about domestic violence issues, and to raise awareness.

- Producing specific information and educational material, for example a publication on the needs of Asian women or on housing options for women and children escaping domestic violence.

- Putting on exhibitions about domestic violence, running roadshows, providing stalls at community events or setting up public meetings, workshops, productions, plays etc.

- Working with schools and the youth service.

E. Engaging in preventative and educational work

- Engaging in preventative work in the education system to assist children and young people to learn that domestic violence is unacceptable in relationships.

- For example, developing education packs on a multi-agency basis for use in schools and youth services and training for youth workers and teachers.

- Developing programmes for male perpetrators of domestic violence, usually in conjunction with probation departments and in liaison with women's services.

- As an active part of prevention work, making it a priority to facilitate increased resources for direct services for women and children, including refuge and outreach provision.

- Engaging in Zero Tolerance campaigns.

8 How to raise the profile of the forum and gain influence locally

To be effective in improving services, domestic violence forums need to become well-known locally and to be able to exert influence.

There are many ways of building credibility and support. For example, a few multi-agency networks are direct campaigning organisations which take an activist stance and concentrate on building community and women's support. Most, however, are concerned specifically with coordinating and improving local policy and practice.

Multi-agency forums need to be known and taken seriously by all relevant local agencies and organisations, including both front-line workers and managers within them, local policy makers, local councillors, women's advocacy and support services and networks, abused women and children and the wider community.

Some ideas on how to gain influence

- Develop a clear identity.

- Develop a local profile among agencies, (at both practitioner and manager level) policy makers, and in all communities in the area.

- Ensure consistency of attendance and commitment from member agencies.

- Try to ensure that agency representatives are delegated by their agency (rather than attending on an ad hoc basis).

- Try to ensure that agency representatives have some influence within their agency (or can access those who do).

- If possible, develop expertise in using local government structures.

- Develop a portfolio of activities and interventions which are visible and which improve local services.

- Engage in publicity exercises.

- Develop skills in local fundraising.

- Support local women's initiatives and liaise with abused women and children, advocates and agencies representing them, and community development programmes.

- Involve local policy makers in the initiative.

How to involve policy makers and senior managers

One of the key strengths of domestic violence forums is their grass-roots dynamism and activism. However the support and commitment of senior policy makers and managers is also required for the initiative to be taken seriously and to gain influence locally. Domestic violence forums may face a dilemma in combining both these aspects of their work.

Policy makers or practitioners? How to resolve this dilemma

Some suggestions

These suggestions are alternative ways of involving policy makers and practitioners. Please note that some of these ideas are not feasible in some areas.

- Involve a mixture of both policy makers and front-line practitioners and 'grass-roots activists' in the initiative in both the full forum and any management body.

- Ensure, if possible, that practitioners who attend the forum have support and commitment from their managers.

- Ensure, if possible, that officers who attend are able to make decisions on behalf of their agency or to access those who can.

- Maintain a grass-roots forum but make contact with, and establish recognised links, with senior managers.

- Maintain a grass-roots forum but hold regular conferences to inform and develop awareness among senior management in a wide range of agencies.

- Maintain a grass-roots forum with a high profile and invite senior managers to the forum from time to time to answer questions, discuss problems and report on progress in their agency.

- Establish regular formal meetings with senior policy makers and managers in each local agency to discuss possible improvements in practice, and to feed into policy discussions .

- Work to establish a corporate response to domestic violence across a local authority into which local domestic violence forums can feed, for example, through establishing a working group of officers across the authority's departments.

- Work to establish a wider multi-agency forum of policy makers and senior managers from all the key local agencies to develop a broad domestic violence strategy across the locality.

Two tier forums

Strategy-making forums of senior policy makers have been set up in some areas. This type of forum may be local authority-wide, county-wide or may fit in with local police or probation areas, with smaller local forums feeding in information and expertise.

The idea of a two tier structure of wider strategy making forums and local practitioner forums is an innovative one. It has yet to be developed fully and has met with limited success to date.

Two tier system will help to:

- Get domestic violence taken seriously at senior management level.

- Increase the possibility of senior managers actively taking part.

- Involve senior policy makers in multi-agency strategy-making bodies on domestic violence, which have real power to make changes.

- Develop a domestic violence strategy across a whole locality.

- Inform such strategy with direct input from practitioners.
- Get commitment from senior managers in each agency. This will also inform domestic violence policy within that individual agency.

Possible difficulties with a two tier system

- Duplication of organisational effort and work done.
- The same officers may end up attending both forums.
- Officers attending the wider forum may be insufficiently senior to effect changes in policy and strategy.
- Senior officers may attend but may have little interest in the topic or may be unable to prioritise the work or to make realistic commitments due to other pressures.
- Senior officers may not 'take on board' information from practitioners and grass-roots agencies.
- Some managers may be cut off from practitioners and from direct service delivery.
- County-wide forums may be less advanced in terms of taking on equality issues than local urban forums.
- Regional or county forums may look good but be largely ineffective in practice.
- They may introduce further bureaucratic layers or 'hoops' through which new initiatives and planned activities have to pass.

Developing a creative and dynamic grass-roots approach, informed by the perspectives of women who have experienced domestic violence and by advocates and activists in the field, while also involving senior policy makers and managers locally, remains a problematic issue for domestic violence multi-agency initiatives.

9   How to resource multi-agency forums

- Most domestic violence forums have no resources of their own.

- Member agencies often share or donate resources and may rotate tasks between them on behalf of the multi-agency initiative.

- In many areas, statutory agencies are likely to have more resources than voluntary ones and may be able to take on duties, such as providing the secretariat.

- However all agencies, including statutory ones, have few resources to spare and most cannot maintain such extra work for long periods.

- Many voluntary sector agencies are not in a position to donate resources, or even to delegate officers to attend.

- While the Women's Aid federations have a national role in the development of policy and practice on multi-agency work and have provided training, support and consultancy to many new and existing multi-agency initiatives, they have no funding to facilitate forums directly.

- Without further resources, it is almost impossible for domestic violence forums to develop and grow beyond basic networking. The 1995 *Home Office Inter-agency Circular* did not contain proposals on resourcing.

Possible sources of funding and resources

- Funding from local authority committees.

- Funding from police authorities.

- Funding from specialist schemes, for example the Home Office Safer Cities scheme or Partnership schemes.

- Special local funding initiatives.

- Building multi-agency domestic violence work into the job descriptions of designated agency officers in each member agency.

- Releasing officers specifically to engage in multi-agency work.

- Utilising specialist employees, for example local authority women's equality or community safety officers, who can sometimes coordinate multi-agency work on domestic violence as part of their jobs. Some Women's Aid groups have obtained funding for a development worker on multi-agency work.

- Redefining domestic violence as a core concern for certain key agencies so that access to resourcing and designated work on domestic violence becomes possible.

- Accessing private funding, for example, through solicitors.

However, a lack of resources is the single largest factor in inhibiting the development of multi-agency work on domestic violence.

Multi-agency coordination and preventative work should go hand in hand with the provision of services. But because of a shortage of resources, domestic violence forums may end up competing for funding with refuges and other emergency services for women and children experiencing domestic violence.

It is good practice to avoid such competition and ensure that Women's' Aid and other refuges and women's services are adequately resourced and able to develop.

Despite these difficulties, some forums have secured funding to employ coordinators and development workers.

10 Employing multi-agency forum personnel: coordinators, development workers and administrators

Employing a coordinator or development worker and other staff is of key importance in progressing the work done by the multi-agency forum.

It is helpful if the forum has already developed guiding principles and aims and objectives to inform the work of the coordinator.

- Sometimes, coordinators or development workers are employees of statutory agencies.

- Sometimes, officers employed within one agency can perform coordination duties for a domestic violence forum as part of a wider job.

- A number of forums employ their own coordinators or development workers.

- In general, employing a coordinator or development workers works best when they are supported by an administrator, at least on a part-time basis, to provide administrative servicing or support.

Domestic violence employees are managed in a variety of ways, but usually either:

- Through a statutory agency, or

- By the forum Steering Committee, or an Employment Sub-group of it, acting as a management committee.

Employee management styles are generally fairly participatory, in keeping with wider ideas in multi-agency domestic violence work about balancing differences between agencies and evolving collective, coordinated practice and policy responses to domestic violence.

Duties of multi-agency coordinators and development workers

The role of a coordinator is to support and facilitate the project, not to lead it. The ideas fuelling the forum ideally need to come from service providers and practitioners rather than from the coordinator, so that the membership, through the Steering Committee if there is one, leads the project. The duties of coordinators are wide-ranging and complex. Development workers often have a similar role; to work with the Steering Committee to develop the forum.

Qualities required for a coordinator or development worker

- Good coordinating and administrative skills.

- Good networking skills, to bring agencies together.

- The ability to act as an 'honest broker' between agencies and interest groups and to smooth out difficulties.

- The ability to work closely with refuges and with women survivors of domestic violence.

- The ability to act as a spokesperson on behalf of abused women and children.

- The ability to work closely with senior managers and policy makers, and the statutory sector as a whole.

- The ability to work closely with grass-roots projects and community groups.

- The ability to promote and publicise the initiative throughout the locality.

- The ability to deal sensitively with issues of equal opportunities.

- A background in women's services or refuges (where possible).

- A developed understanding of the gendered power dynamics of domestic violence.

11 Statutory agencies and multi-agency work

- It is vital that all relevant statutory agencies participate in multi-agency work, if it is to succeed.

- Further guidance and advice on this issue from relevant ministries would be of assistance.

- Commitment from both senior managers and practitioners is required to enable new multi-agency initiatives to go forward.

- At the moment, officers often attend in a rather ad hoc way. A better practice is for officers to attend as official representatives their agency.

- Mechanisms need to be in place for delegated officers to report back, and for their agency to be able to respond to initiatives from the forum in order to develop improved policy and practice.

Points to be aware of:

Statutory agencies need to be:

- aware of their power vis à vis the voluntary sector and independent women's services.

- willing to work out ways of working collectively with other agencies.

- able to respect differences in approach and philosophy, and in resourcing.

The police

- Police involvement in multi-agency domestic violence projects is essential.

- The police have engaged in increasing amounts of multi-agency work on domestic violence in recent years.

- Sensitive multi-agency work has been conducted by the police in various areas. This is particularly the case where police domestic violence units or domestic violence officer posts are in existence.

- The police are often involved at both a practitioner and policy level.

- Domestic violence initiatives quite often have the support of very senior officers.

- Police practice, encouraged by Home Office guidance, can be a model in these respects.

- In some areas, the police have developed good practice guidance in consultation with the local domestic violence forum.

- However, there are some problems with police involvement in multi-agency domestic violence forums in terms of police power, disagreements between the police and other agencies on occasion, criticism from some agencies of potentially aggressive or racist policing and also of police culture in relation to race and gender issues and domestic violence. (For a discussion of these issues see Patel, P. 'The multi-agency approach to domestic violence: A panacea or obstacle to women's struggles for freedom from violence', (in Harwin, Malos and Hague (forthcoming)).

Local authority departments

- Social services and housing departments are involved in many domestic violence forums.

- Nevertheless, they are also absent in a surprisingly large number of cases, given their key involvement in domestic violence work.

- Often, basic grade officers attend with little support from their department or from senior officers.

- It is essential that managers and policy makers are involved in, and committed to, multi-agency domestic violence initiatives.

- Managers can then support practitioners who attend forums and can make sure that policy and practice issues are taken up within their departments (or on a multi-agency basis).

- In some areas, specific policy and practice guidance has been developed in conjunction with domestic violence forums in both social services and housing departments (for example, on the homelessness legislation in relation to domestic violence).

- Within social services, such policies may take the form of child protection and domestic violence policies and guidance on working with the children of women experiencing domestic violence. Some social services departments also have general policy and practice guidelines about domestic violence in place.

- Domestic violence may also be a feature of community care plans and children's services plans with multi-agency involvement.

- With management commitment, social services and housing departments can make important contributions to domestic violence forums and to the evolution of a coordinated response.

- Education departments are seldom involved in domestic violence forums but their commitment is also required, particularly in terms of preventative work in schools and the development of education packs, and of sensitivity to the needs of children living with domestic violence.

Local authority special units

- Local authority special units, where they exist, are frequently key participants in multi-agency initiatives, and sometimes initiators.

- These are most usually community safety units, women's or equality units.

- Such units are sometimes able to provide coordination and other services for local forums.

- Domestic violence multi-agency forums may then be able to feed into a wider crime prevention or equal opportunities strategy, and to exchange ideas and expertise with other multi-agency groups engaged in community safety or equalities work.

The probation service

- Following on from the Association of Chief Officers of Probation (ACOP) Statement on domestic violence (1992, updated 1996), the Probation Service is quite often involved in multi-agency domestic violence work. A National Association of Probation Officers (NAPO) working party is drawing up a statement on domestic violence, including standards for perpetrators projects.

- As for local authority departments, basic grade officers may attend with little support from management.

- Commitment to multi-agency work on domestic violence from managers and policy-making officers is essential.

- Some probation offices have developed practice guidance on domestic violence, alongside domestic violence forums.

- Probation officers are most often involved where there is a local perpetrators programme associated with the initiative or, sometimes, through the court welfare service.

Legal and court personnel

- Private solicitors' firms quite are often active in multi-agency forums, and can sometimes feed information into their professional societies and networks.

- The crown prosecution service has a policy statement on domestic violence and participates in some forums.

- Judges, magistrates, legal and court officers are involved far less.

- The involvement of these officers is essential if a coordinated response to domestic violence is to be built across the criminal justice system.

- Some multi-agency forums have developed specific training for judges, magistrates and court officers and established support projects for women using the criminal justice service.

Health services and health care providers

- Health care providers, for example, health visitors, nurse managers and accident and emergency staff, are involved in some multi-agency initiatives.

- Some health services are involved through community care plans.

- However, representation from health agencies is noticeably poor across the country.

- Greater involvement in, and commitment from, health services and health professionals in multi-agency work on domestic violence is needed as a matter of some urgency.

- Some health workers are involved in drawing up procedures and protocols for working with women experiencing domestic violence and their children.

12 The voluntary sector, Victim Support and multi-agency work

National voluntary organisations

- The four national Women's Aid federations take a role in developing policy and practice on multi-agency responses to domestic violence nationally, and offer consultancy, training and support where possible.

- Some other national voluntary organisations are represented on multi-agency domestic violence forums and their involvement is encouraged.

- Such organisations can usefully develop policy and practice guidance both on domestic violence and on multi-agency work for member groups.

Victim Support

- Nationally, Victim Support has been pro-active in encouraging multi-agency work on domestic violence.

- Local Victim Support groups often take an active, and sometimes leading role, depending on the level of their resources.

Voluntary sector agencies

- Voluntary sector agencies are represented on most, but not all domestic violence forums, leading to an unbalanced response.

- In some initiatives, the voluntary sector participates in the forum but is under-represented on steering committees leading to an imbalance with the statutory sector.

- The involvement of voluntary sector agencies needs to be supported by their management bodies.

- Voluntary sector agencies need to 'sign up' to multi-agency initiatives and to make a recognisable and stated commitment.

- Voluntary sector organisations also need to be open-minded about multi-agency possibilities and about statutory agencies.

- Power differences between statutory and voluntary sector agencies may deter voluntary organisations from participating.

- Statutory sector agencies need to make space for voluntary sector organisations to take part.

- The tendency for statutory sector agencies to 'take over' or to 'own' the work done needs to be counteracted. One approach to this problem is to have strategies to avoid the marginalisation of small voluntary or community groups. For example, positive measures need to adopted to ensure that voluntary sector projects feel welcomed, involved and listened to.

- Some community or women's organisations, for example small groups of black or disabled women, may feel particularly pushed to one side in big multi-agency groups. In such situations, equality issues need to be addressed.

13 Involving Women's Aid and the refuge movement

Women's Aid and other refuge and advocacy services are the key specialist agencies in domestic violence work. Therefore they are also key to the development of multi-agency work.

- However, while Women's Aid and refuge-based advocacy and support services are of central importance in multi-agency work, they are small and under-funded organisations. As a result, they are often overlooked and marginalised within multi-agency initiatives.

- Power differences, and differences in philosophy between refuges and larger agencies, can militate against constructive co-operation.

- Refuge groups may be unable to participate actively or consistently due to constant pressure of crisis work and other demands on their time and energy.

- The ideas and beliefs of refuges may be diluted beyond recognition by other agencies in multi-agency work (especially when 'the lowest common denominator' is the usual style of operation).

- The participation of a refuge group may provide credibility to an multi-agency forum, while the refuge group concerned may in fact be relatively powerless to influence the multi-agency process.

- Where refuge groups are strong and long-established, they may have a powerful voice in multi-agency forums.

- As the only specialist agency, some refuges may do more than their fair share of the work in order to keep an initiative going, perhaps with very few resources.

- Multi-agency work may create a further demand for services which local refuges cannot meet due to poor resources.

- Setting up multi-agency initiatives where refuges remain very poorly resourced can be seen, in some circumstances, as counter-productive.

Strategies for involving Women's Aid and other refuges in a central position in multi-agency work

These need to aim for:

- Recognition by statutory and voluntary sector agencies of the key role played by Women's Aid, refuges and women's advocacy services in domestic violence multi-agency work.

- Acknowledgement by other agencies in the forum and by the forum itself of the expertise and experience of Women's Aid and other refuge groups.

- Recognition by statutory and voluntary sector agencies of the difficulties for refuges which militate against their full participation.

- Recognition in multi or single agency domestic violence policies and in practice guidance of the important role of refuge services.

- The provision of support for refuges and other small community or voluntary sector women's organisations to facilitate their full involvement in multi-agency initiatives.

- An increase in the level of priority placed on multi-agency work by some Women's Aid groups and other refuges.

- The further development by the Women's Aid federations of guidelines, advice and wider strategy to inform the involvement of refuges in multi-agency initiatives.

- Consultation with the Women's Aid federations who can then make contributions and provide support.

- The placing of Women's Aid or other refuge services in positions of power and of management within multi-agency forums as an agreed principle of their operation.

- Possibly reserve positions on steering committees or other management bodies for Women's Aid or other refuges.

Another possibility is for Women's Aid or other refuges to formally take the position of chair of the domestic violence initiative. Several forums have adopted the strategy of reserving the chair of the forum, or specified places on the management or steering committee, for Women's Aid and other refuge groups as a matter of agreed practice.

Advantages and possible disadvantages to this strategy

Advantages

Refuges and women's support services occupy a powerful position within the forum.

Their specialist expertise can assist the forum to develop.

The general Women's Aid perspective on empowering women and children who are experiencing domestic violence and on listening to their voices can inform the forum and all the work done.

Possible disadvantages

Women's Aid and other refuge groups providing refuge and support services may not have the spare time or resources to be involved in such a central way, especially if all workers are engaged in direct crisis work with abused women and children.

If the local refuge group is in the chair, another refuge officer may have to attend to represent the organisation, adding a further pressure.

Women's Aid and other refuge groups may not have the resources to do the extra administrative work which accompanies a central role. In some forums, this work is undertaken by statutory agencies to reduce the load on the refuge group which remains as chair.

However, the participation of refuges and women's independent advocacy services is recognised as of vital importance to a multi-agency forum.

Where they are able to take a central and powerful role, multi-agency work is in general enhanced.

The viability of domestic violence forums which are established without appropriate Women's Aid and refuge involvement is questionable, where such groups exist in the locality.

What happens if there is no refuge in the area?

Where there are no local refuges and few voluntary sector projects which deal with domestic violence, developing multi-agency work may be hindered.

In such situations, difficulties may be experienced in maintaining the centrality of the perspective of abused women. Care should also be taken not to raise expectations of services and public awareness before being clear on how support and resources will be offered to abused women and children and how their safety will be ensured.

Independent women's services to provide refuge, advocacy and support are needed which are not linked to statutory responsibilities. Where there is no refuge, guidance on multi-agency tasks which can be taken on in these circumstances, and on how to maintain a woman-centred and effective approach, may be available from:

- The Women's Aid federations.

- Neighbouring forums or refuges.

- Established forums in other areas.

- Multi-agency training programmes and consultants.

Over many years, the Women's Aid federations have been involved in training and support on establishing refuges and on the development of refuge provision. They can provide consultation and publications on setting up independent locally-based refuge and advocacy services where these do not exist.

14 Involving women who have experienced domestic violence

- Women who have experienced domestic violence are seldom involved in multi-agency initiatives in their own right, although they may attend as professionals or representatives of other agencies.

- Many abused women and others involved in multi-agency work feel, however, that forums should listen to the views of women and children who have experienced domestic violence and learn from them.

- The 'bottom' line in terms of informal accountability of multi-agency initiatives is to increase the safety of abused women and children.

- Women survivors of domestic violence are the experts on their own experience. Therefore it is vital that they are consulted and involved in multi-agency work.

- Some women who have experienced domestic violence feel happy to attend forum meetings in order to express the views of survivors, but many do not wish to make such a public statement or public commitment.

- There are also issues of confidentiality, of power differences, and of conflicts and complexities between the professional and 'service user' role.

- Abused women often give their free time and expertise to domestic violence initiatives. Strategies need to be in place so that women are not used or exploited if they become involved. There are many ways of achieving this. For example, by payment, exchange in kind, reimbursement of expenses, crèche and refreshment provision.

However, new practice is now developing to facilitate:

- The involvement or participation of domestic violence survivors in multi-agency forums.

- Informal accountability of domestic violence forums to abused women and children.

Two key suggestions

- Women's Aid and other refuges taking a more pro-active role in the involvement of domestic violence survivors.

- Setting up advisory or monitoring groups of domestic violence survivors

Women's Aid and other refuges taking a more pro-active role

Refuges could take a significantly more pro-active role than they do currently, as a matter of principle and of agreed strategy in terms of:

- Facilitating the involvement of abused women and children in multi-agency policy making through refuge, follow-up and outreach services.

- Passing information and ideas between multi-agency domestic violence forums and abused women and children.

- Providing information on multi-agency issues for women and children experiencing domestic violence.

- Discussing multi-agency initiatives at meetings with abused women and children (eg, house meetings, residents' meetings, children's meetings, support group or self-help group meetings etc).

Guidance for refuge services on these issues from the Women's Aid federations could be of assistance.

Advantages and possible disadvantages of this approach

Advantages	Possible Disadvantages
Abused women gain access to information about multi-agency work and can contribute to strategy and policy making through refuge personnel.	There are clear resource implications in expecting refuges to take on a new role in terms of facilitating multi-agency work.
Even if women are not interested in multi-agency work or do not feel able to take on an active role while living in the crisis situation of a refuge; the information is available.	Refuge staff may already be over-loaded and over-worked.
Women's Aid and other refuge services already have policies of listening to women who have experienced domestic violence and representing their interests, views and needs. They also have a history of providing independent advocacy for abused women and children. The active involvement of refuges as a 'bridge' between abused women and multi-agency initiatives is therefore fitting and also achievable.	Women who have experienced domestic violence may feel pressured to be part of a forum while they are living in a crisis situation.
	Confidentiality issues can be difficult unless sensitive procedures to protect women are in place.
Information and participation is democratised and made more open.	Refuges only represent a proportion of women and children experiencing domestic violence (even if follow-up and outreach services are included).

Setting up advisory or monitoring groups of domestic violence survivors

These groups, consisting of women who have experienced domestic violence, are set up in order to discuss, monitor and advise on all aspects of the structure, working practices and activities of multi-agency domestic violence forums. They represent a new development in multi-agency work.

Advantages	Possible Disadvantages
Domestic violence forums are more accountable to women experiencing domestic violence.	There can be problems in setting up and maintaining a group of this type.
All the work of the forum is monitored and 'overseen' by the advisory group.	There can be clear difficulties in terms of equal opportunities in setting up an ad hoc and possibly unrepresentative survivors group.
Such groups are innovative and creative.	

Practice is currently involving in this respect and initiatives seeking to engage in such work may be able to seek further advice from those who have already done so.

Further ideas

To facilitate involvement and accountability, women who have experienced domestic violence and their children could:

- Make use of, and contribute to, improved publicity and awareness-raising material about multi-agency projects and the work they do about domestic violence and about refuges and other available services.

- Make use of, and contribute to, specialist resource directories and information packs for women and children experiencing domestic violence to use. These are sometimes produced in local areas with details of services, of advice and information lines and of multi-agency activities.

- Fill out questionnaires and participate in other methods to pass information to local forums.

- Be involved in drawing up and writing publicity material, leaflets, information packs etc.

- Make a formal input into the design and delivery of domestic violence training programmes.

- Participate in the design, setting-up and running of new services for abused women and children.

- Participate in the design, writing, agreeing, implementing and monitoring of domestic violence policies and good practice guidance by agencies and domestic violence forums.

- Have access to a specially established local domestic violence 'ombudsman'.

These suggestions have been put forward by women survivors of domestic violence.

In parallel with the suggestions on the previous page and in addition to other work discussed earlier, domestic violence forums could:

- Attempt to improve publicity and produce awareness raising material which is of direct use to abused women and children.

- Facilitate the direct involvement of domestic violence survivors in this work, as a matter of agreed principle.

- Facilitate and raise funds for survivors groups, for outreach work, and for specific follow-up, advocacy and outreach work conducted by Women's Aid and other refuges, for example, with women and children who have moved on from refuges, or with specific groups of women and children, for instance from minority ethnic communities.

Such work could benefit abused women and children and also provide improved consultation.

15 Equalities issues and multi-agency work

Equalities work is a vital part of multi-agency coordination in order to provide services for all who require them.

However, developing equal opportunities on a multi-agency basis is a difficult task. Member agencies vary as to how much work they have done on this issue.

Some suggestions for developing an equalities perspective in multi-agency forums

- Make equal opportunities an integral part of all activities.

- Integrate equalities issues into all the structures and practices of the multi-agency forum.

- Try to build a varied membership of both organisations and individuals on a principled basis in order to achieve good representation across the forum.

- Ensure that membership of the steering group or management body of the forum reflects this diversity.

- Ensure that representatives from various minority groups or communities are in positions of power within the initiative.

- Take active measures to combat the marginalisation of some groups or organisations.

- Make meetings welcoming to different groups.

- Produce equal opportunities policies which are regularly reviewed and developed.

- Set up specialist equalities sub-groups to undertake specific pieces of equalities work.

- Possibly set up an equalities advisory or monitoring group to advise and monitor the forum's work in terms of equal opportunities (this group would not need to consist of forum members).

- Possibly set up specialist advisory or monitoring groups (eg, consisting of black women or disabled women specifically).

- Produce specific literature and resource material (eg, for lesbians or for disabled women who have experienced domestic violence).

- Translate materials into local community languages and into different formats (eg, onto audio-tape and into large print).

- Include such translation and interpreting services in all funding applications.

- Include equalities issues as an integral part of all domestic violence training offered.

- Offer specialist training on equalities issues to both forum and steering group members, as well as to other agencies and the public.

- Use venues which are fully accessible in all respects for all forum activities.

- Conduct outreach work about domestic violence and the work of the forum (eg, in minority ethnic communities).

- Use good equalities practice in regard to recruitment and selection.

- Identify particular, unmet needs of specific groups (eg, children, black women, older women etc) through research and consultation.

- Initiate new projects to meet these needs.

- Provide consultants, support groups or other support structures, to offer specific support on equalities issues for steering groups or forum members from minority groups and communities.

16 What makes a multi-agency forum effective?

To be successful, multi-agency forums need to monitor and evaluate their work in terms of:

- Effectiveness in meeting and in highlighting the needs of women and children experiencing domestic violence.

- Effectiveness of the structures, decision making, organisational procedures and processes.

However, effectiveness is hard to measure in terms of increasing the safety of abused women and children, reducing domestic violence and responding to its impact.

Forums may be able to develop their own measures of effectiveness related specifically to their local situation.

Some factors which contribute to an effective forum

- Active involvement of statutory agencies at both practitioner and policy-making level, with senior management support.

- Full participation of Women's Aid and independent refuge and advocacy services, and concrete strategies to actively promote their central involvement.

- Active participation of community, women's and grass-roots organisations.

- Active involvement of the voluntary sector at practitioner and at management level.

- Consistent, committed and active attendance and membership, preferably with members delegated to attend by their agency as an agreed part of their work duties or job description.

- Stated commitment from member agencies, followed up by action, so that policy and practice changes can be taken up actively and implemented both within and between agencies.

- Adoption of guiding principles and the development of common agreements about domestic violence.

- Clear and well-developed aims and objectives, equal opportunity policies and other terms of reference

- A workable structure enabling clarity and lines of accountability but avoiding layers of bureaucracy.

- Resources for activities, projects and coordination work, and for servicing the forum.

- If possible, the employment of a coordinator or development worker with administrative support.

- Relating all activities to meet the needs, and increase the safety, of abused women and children and decrease domestic violence.

- The development of concrete initiatives and activities which are within the capabilities of the forum.

- The integration of equalities issues into the forum's work.

- The involvement of, and some form of informal accountability to, women survivors of domestic violence and their children.

- Evaluation and monitoring in relation to work done and its effectiveness.

17 Smoke-screen or creative way forward?

Multi-agency work is now seen as the way forward in tackling domestic violence, together with the provision of basic services. The establishment of domestic violence forums marks an innovative development which has given rise to new opportunities for service coordination and for preventative work.

However:

- Multi-agency work can appear as a smoke-screen or as a way of saving face and disguising inaction, unless it is positioned within a supportive policy and practice framework at both local and central government level.

- For this to happen, further local and national guidance is required from government departments, from statutory agencies, from the national Women's Aid federations and from other national bodies.

- Resourcing is also required to avoid a piecemeal, ad hoc approach and competition between direct services and multi-agency work for limited funding.

- Multi-agency coordination cannot be effective if the services to be coordinated are lacking or under-resourced and facing cut-backs.

- Where multi-agency initiatives go hand-in-hand with the provision of refuges and other services and where they undertake effective coordination and preventative, educational and awareness-raising work, they can provide an innovative and creative 'next step' in combating and preventing domestic violence.

References

Association of Chief Officers of Probation (1992, revised 1996) *Position statement on domestic violence*, London: ACOP.

Dominy, N. and Radford, L. (1996) *Domestic violence in Surrey: Developing an effective inter-agency response*, Roehampton: Surrey County Council and Roehampton Institute.

Dublin Women's Aid (1995) *Discussion document on an inter-agency approach to domestic violence*, Dublin: Dublin Women's Aid.

Government Reply to the Third Report from the Home Affairs Committee (1993) Session 1992-93, HC245, London: HMSO.

Hague, G. and Malos, E. (1993) *Domestic violence: Action for change*, Cheltenham: New Clarion Press.

Hague, G., Malos, E. and Dear, W. (1995a) *Against domestic violence: Inter-agency initiatives*, SAUS Working Paper 127, Bristol: SAUS Publications.

Hague, G., Malos, E. and Dear, W. (1996) *Multi-agency work and domestic violence: A national study of inter-agency initiatives*, Bristol: The Policy Press.

Harwin, N., Malos, E. and Hague, G. (eds) (forthcoming) *Inter-agency responses and domestic violence*, London: Whiting and Birch.

Home Affairs Committee, (1993) *Inquiry into domestic violence*, London: HMSO.

Home Office (1990) *Circular 60/90, Domestic violence*, London: Home Office.

Home Office (1995) *Inter-agency Circular: Inter-agency co-ordination to tackle domestic violence*, London: Home Office and Welsh Office.

Liddle, M. and Gelsthorpe, L. (1994a) *Inter-agency crime prevention: Organising local delivery*, Police Research Group, Crime Prevention Unit Series, Paper 52, London: Home Office.

Liddle, M. and Gelsthorpe, L. (1994b) *Crime prevention and inter-agency co-operation*, Police Research Group, Crime Prevention Unit Series, Paper 53, London: Home Office.

Liddle, M. and Gelsthorpe, L. (1994c) *Inter-agency crime prevention: further issues*, Police Research Group, Crime Prevention Unit Series, Supplementary Paper to Papers 52 and 53, London: Home Office.

London Borough of Islington (1995b) *Stop: striving to prevent domestic violence: An activity pack for working with children and young people*, London: London Borough of Islington.

Mama, A., (1989) *The hidden struggle: Statutory and voluntary responses to violence against black women in the home*, London: London Race and Housing Research Unit.

National Inter-Agency Working Party Report (1992) *Domestic Violence*, London: Victim Support.

Pence, E. and Paymar, M. (1990) *Power and control: Tactics of men who batter - an educational curriculum*, Duluth, Minnesota: Duluth Abuse Intervention Project.

Sampson, A., Smith, D., Pearson, G., Blagg, H. and Stubbs, P. (1991) 'Gender issues in inter-agency relations: police, probation and social services' in P. Abbott and C. Wallace (eds), *Gender, power and sexuality*, London: MacMillan.

Sampson, A., Stubbs, P., Smith, D., Pearson, G. and Blagg. H. (1988) 'Crime, localities and the multi-agency approach', *British Journal of Criminology*, vol 28, pp 478-493.

Smith, L. (1989) *Domestic violence: An overview of the literature*, Home Office Research Studies, No. 107, London: HMSO.

Appendix 1

Extract from Terms of Reference of a local domestic violence forum

Policy statement/principles

1. Domestic violence is defined by the Forum as:
   The emotional, physical, sexual or psychological abuse of a person by their partner, family member or someone with whom there is, or has been, a relationship.

2. Members of this Forum accept that domestic violence is a serious crime which is unacceptable to society, and that all individuals have a right to live their lives free of abuse and/or the threat of violence.

3. The Forum has adopted a holistic approach to the prevention of domestic violence which involves increasing the availability of protection and support offered to survivors as well as access to help for perpetrators.

4. The Forum acknowledges that domestic violence essentially involves the misuse of power and the exercise of control by one person, usually a man, over another, usually a woman. The two are, or have been, in some intimate relationship with each other.

5. The work of the Forum is informed by the experiences of survivors of domestic violence which indicates it involves a range of different types of abuse which may include severe physical assault, rape and sexual abuse, and mental/emotional abuse involving degradation, humiliation, verbal abuse, threats and withholding money.

6. Any women or child can be abused, irrespective of race, class, age, religion, sexuality, mental or physical ability.

7. Members of the Forum also acknowledge there are many reasons why women stay in abusive relationships which may include fear, love, financial dependency, isolation, religion or children. No one deserves to be abused. Often a woman wants the violence to stop but not the relationship to end. The personal relationship between the abused person and the perpetrator of the violence must always be considered.

8. The Forum recognises that the non-judgmental models of working with domestic violence developed by the women's voluntary sector (eg, Women's Aid, Rape Crisis) are crucial in helping to meet the needs of abused women and their children.

9. Members of the Forum accept that:
   Domestic violence requires an inter-agency response involving coordination and collaboration of a range of social, legal, financial and health resources. This Forum aims to work towards the development of a common policy and best practice to enable and empower people to live their lives free of violence.

Mission statement

1. It is the intention of the Forum to bring about social change with regard to domestic violence, the treatment of people experiencing domestic violence and the treatment of perpetrators.

2. Our mission statement is as follows:

   To achieve the general acceptance that domestic violence is a crime and unacceptable to society, to ensure that support is given to people experiencing domestic violence and help for perpetrators is readily available and accessible.

Procedural guidelines

1. Membership of the Forum is open to any interested group, organisation or individual willing to adhere to the terms of reference and equal opportunities policy and to assist the Forum in progressing its aims.

2. The Forum is expected to meet a minimum of four times per annum.

3. The Forum meetings will be chaired by the coordinator.

4. All members are expected to participate on sub-committees or working parties established to achieve strategic objectives and progress the aims of the group.

5. Particular reference should be made to the equal opportunities policy in all aspects of work undertaken by the Forum.

6. Members of the Forum should seek to address the role and position of all women in society in all aspects of work undertaken.

Equal opportunities policy

1. *Statement.* The Forum is committed to equal opportunities and treatment for all regardless of gender, race, colour, ethnic or national origin, religion, disability, age, appearance, marital status or sexuality. We recognise that many groups are disadvantaged in our society and we will seek to actively assist disadvantaged groups to participate in our work and benefit from our services.

2. *Membership.* Membership of the Forum is open to representatives from any interested group. All members are expected to uphold group policy, and no member will be treated less favourably than other persons because of their gender, race, colour, ethnic or national origin, religion, disability, age, appearance, marital status or sexuality. We will actively seek to ensure that disadvantaged minority groups are represented on the Forum.

3. *Targeting services.* The Forum recognises that in the vast majority of cases, it is women who are the victims of domestic violence from known men. We also acknowledge that women are a disadvantaged group who have less income, housing, transport and other services. We therefore choose to target our services specifically at women. We acknowledge that men too experience domestic violence, and endeavour to support services for men provided these do not in any way diminish service provision for women, eg, by competing for scarce resources. The Forum will actively assist disadvantaged minority groups to benefit from its services. We will seek to identify the needs of minority groups, especially black and disabled women, and establish close relationships with these groups. We will collect and monitor records of those who use services for victims of domestic violence and take steps to improve accessibility of services to disadvantaged groups who are under-represented.

4. *Employment.* As an employer, the Forum will ensure that no job applicant or employee receives less favourable treatment on the grounds of gender, race, colour, ethnic or national origin, religion, disability, age, appearance, marital status or sexuality (except where allowed under the law and is necessary). In addition, we will seek actively to encourage applications from minority groups in order to achieve equality of opportunity. Interview and appointment procedures shall be adopted so as to minimise any disadvantage suffered by any minority group.

Appendix 2

Selected examples of existing domestic violence forums' sub-groups

Examples of multi-agency forum sub-groups in operation in 1996

Finance

Fundraising

Employment (ie, to manage any workers)

Training

Legal issues

Support in using the criminal justice service

Housing issues

Children's needs

Working with children

Youth and education work

Publicity

Zero Tolerance

Equalities

Anti-oppressive practice

Issues for Asian women

Issues for back women and children

Issues for disabled women and children

Working with abused women

Working with abusive men

Examples of sub-groups managing specific projects

Help-lines and advice lines

Drop-in centres

Perpetrators projects

Survivors support projects

Specific research projects

Youth and education projects

Examples of sub-groups organising specific work on a 'one off' basis

Organising a conference or seminar

Producing a directory of services

Producing a leaflet or booklet

Producing multi-agency practice guidance

Producing an education pack for use in schools and youth clubs

Setting up a refuge or support centre

Appendix 3

Useful addresses

Assistance in conducting multi-agency work on domestic violence is available from the Women's Aid federations, a few training consultants, some domestic violence researchers and established domestic violence forums.

The 1995 Home Office Inter-agency Circular, Inter-agency Co-ordination to tackle Domestic Violence, is available from:

Action Against Crime Unit
Home Office
50, Queen Anne's Gate
London SW1H 0AT
Tel: (0171) 273-2625

Contact information for the Women's Aid federations:

WAFE
The Women's Aid Federation (England)
PO Box 391
Bristol BS99 7WS
Tel: (0117) 944-4411

WAFE National Helpline Tel: (0117) 963-3542

Welsh Women's Aid
Cardiff Office
38-48 Crwys Road
Cardiff CF2 4NN
Tel: (01222) 390874

Aberystwyth Office
4 Pound Place
Aberystwyth
Tel: (01970) 612748

Rhyl Office
26 Wellington Street
Rhyl
Clwyd LL18 1BN
Tel: (01745) 334767

Scottish Women's Aid
12 Torphichen Street
Edinburgh,
Scotland EH3 8JQ
Tel: (0131) 221 0401

Northern Ireland Women's Aid
129 University Street
Belfast
Northern Ireland BT7 1HP
Tel: (01232) 249041

Women's Aid Helpline in Northern Ireland
Tel (01232) 331818